JADE-SKY

SPIRIT
SIGNS

Understanding
Signs in your Everyday Life

BLUE ANGEL®
PUBLISHING

Spirit Signs

This printing 2020

Published by Blue Angel Publishing
80 Glen Tower Drive, Glen Waverley,
Victoria, Australia 3150
E-mail: info@blueangelonline.com
Website: www.blueangelonline.com

Edited by Tanya Graham

Blue Angel is a registered trademark of Blue Angel Gallery Pty. Ltd.

ISBN: 978-1-922161-46-8

*"It all depends on how we look at things,
and not on how they are themselves."*

C. G. Jung

INTRODUCTION

Understanding Signs in your Everyday Life

Everything happens for a reason – there are no coincidences in life. Whether you are consciously aware of it or not, your day-to-day world is teeming with signs from the Universe, designed to guide you through your life and support you in all that you do.

You do not need to be a psychic medium to receive signs from the Universe or from your passed loved ones and guides in spirit. Each and every one of us can experience signs and receive their own personal guidance from the Universe – it's just a matter of learning to recognise them.

What is a sign?
A sign is something that occurs in your life to get you to take notice or to deliver a message to you from your spirit guides or passed loved ones. A sign can also serve as a kind of flag or a helpful hint to highlight where you need to go or who you need to connect with. There is a multitude of different types of signs and reasons why a person may need to experience or receive a sign from the spirit world.

How do I know what a sign is?

It can be tricky at first trying to learn how to work out what is a sign and what is not. A big thing to look out for when looking for signs is the synchronicity of how things fit together.

An interesting way to think about signs is to look at each one as an individual thread of string. One piece of string on its own is not very strong, but if you weave multiple pieces of string together they can form a strong length of rope. It is the same with signs: one sign on its own may not seem particularly significant, but when you begin to notice multiple signs pointing you in the same direction, you'll naturally take more notice and it will become easier to see whatever it is that spirit is trying to show you. Sometimes your spirit guides can deliver a message with three different signs meaning the same thing.

Can anything be a sign?

Yes, there are many different signs out there so, in theory, everything could be a sign. But if you start interpreting every little thing that happens as a potential sign, you could become distracted from the most important and significant signs being offered to you. Whenever you have a doubt, simply ask for further confirmation or dig a bit deeper. For example, if the lights keep turning themselves on and off in your home, it might be wise to check if there is a problem with the wiring. If you check and there is no fault, you can be sure it is spirit trying to connect with you or get your attention.

Do signs always have to be out of the ordinary?
Can signs come in different ways or are they always the same way?
No, they do not have to be out of the ordinary, some of the best signs are everyday occurrences like finding a coin on the ground or hearing a certain song on the radio. You do not need a big genie jumping out of its bottle; sometimes it is easier for spirit to communicate with you through more accessible everyday objects. Once you begin to understand what a sign is, spirit will often continue to use that same sign to get a message to you as well as offering other signs in different circumstances.

Who gives us signs?
Signs come from the spirit world and the Universe. They can be from your passed loved ones, spirit guides, angels, ascended masters and other deities.

Can I ask for my passed loved ones to send me signs?
Yes, most definitely, you can ask for help any time from your passed loved ones, spirit guides and angels. All you need to do is consciously ask in your mind. You can ask for specific signs, but always be open to other signs that come through too. Sometimes your loved ones and guides could be sending you various signs, but if you are too focused on receiving a sign in a particular form, you might miss the other great signs they send.

Number 0's

Connection, Manifestation, Eternity

It is always a powerful sign when you see the number 0 or 0 repeated such as 000. The number zero relates to your connection with the Universal energy. In ancient times the number 0 was associated with the 'God's source.'

000 is a powerful sign to remind you to keep open spiritually and to let you know that you are at one with the Universe. You are not a separate entity; everything is connected in the circle of life, and there is no beginning or end.

Number 0 or 000 is also a sign to let you know that you can manifest what you want in life, you just have to keep positive and follow your own intuition. Remember, you are a very powerful person: when you are trying to manifest something, it's very important that you focus on the positive things that you want to occur; don't focus on the negative things. Trust that you will find the answers that you need.

The shape of the number 0 is also significant because the circle has traditionally been a symbol that represents eternity and going 'full circle'. That is why people in relationships often wear rings as a symbol of commitment.

Number 1's, 11:11

Confirmation, New beginnings, Synchronicity

11:11 means that spirit is with you; it is time to notice that they are around guiding, comforting and protecting you. You will often see 11:11 when you're on the verge of making a big life change or decision. 11:11 also appears when you are experiencing a lot of synchronicity in the happenings and events in your life. It means your spirit guides and angels are near.

When you see the number sequence 111 or 11:11, this is also a very powerful time for you to be clear about what you do want. Focus on manifesting positive things in your life because this is a golden time for you to make a wish.

The number 1 is also associated with new beginnings, new cycles, success and leadership – many people strive to be 'number 1' in their chosen field.

If we add up the numbers in 11:11, we find it also relates to the number 4 which is all about balance. When you see this number it is a huge sign that you are on the right track and it can also let you know that you are going through a time of spiritual awakening.

Number 2's, 222

Balance, Positivity, Partnerships

The number 2 is a balanced and grounded number. It is a very positive sign to see 222 or 2222; when you see this number two repeating in this way, it is all about trusting in the Universe, keeping the faith and knowing that you are going to be OK.

Your life purpose is also associated with the number 222 or 2222. If these numbers keep popping up for you it may be time for you to look at what your life's purpose is. There may be new opportunities around you right now. Dedicate some time to thinking about what you have been working on or trying to manifest, or what you intuitively feel you should be doing. 222 is a sign that if you keep manifesting positively, your hopes and dreams will come true for you at the right time and this will also open up a positive new cycle in your life.

The number 2 represents partnerships or pairs – you are not alone, your spirit guides, passed loved ones and angels are with you. The number 2 also takes us away from being by ourselves, feeling lonely or being driven by ego to be number one.

Number 3's, 333

Angels, Spirit guides, Triple trinity

The number 3 has traditionally been connected with many different spiritual and religious beliefs. One example is the Roman Catholic 'holy trinity': father/mother/child; another is the pagan trinity of the maiden/the mother/the crone. The number 3 also represents the three aspects of a person: the mind, body and soul. When you notice the number 3 becoming prominent in your life, it's a sign to pay attention to the balance of these three aspects in yourself. Focusing too strongly on any one of them, at the expense of the others, can lead to imbalance which can impact your happiness, health and general wellbeing.

The number 333 resonates with the same energies of the number 3 except the potency is tripled, making it even more powerful. If you see the number sequence 333 it is a strong sign to let you know that you are surrounded by extra angels, spirit guides and ascended masters at this time. They are all with you, supporting you and confirming that you are on exactly the right path. If you aren't sure what your right path is, they will help you to see the truth of the situation and move forwards.

Number 4's, 444

Security, Strong foundations, Hard work

The number 4 is double the number 2; it gives you extra strength, grounding and balance. If you look at many different customs and traditions around the world, the number 4 is very significant. It represents the four directions: North, South, East and West. It also represents the four seasons: Summer, Autumn, Winter and Spring and the four elements: Earth, Air, Wind and Fire. There are also four phases of the moon. It's no coincidence that all of these important aspects of our world come in fours. It is all about balancing everything out, having equal energy in each area.

Number 4 is a productive and positive sign – it means that all the hard work you have done will pay off for you. The 444 sequence triples the energy of the number 4 which focuses on doing things the right way, putting the hard work in and building secure foundations for the future.

444 around you is a great indicator that everything is in balance. It's also a very powerful sign to let you know that you are on the right path. Keep going, your spirit guides and angels are with you.

Number 5's, 555

Change, Transformation, New energy

Prepare for imminent new opportunities, transformation and change when you see the number sequence 555. The number sequence 555 is an important sign because the number 5 represents change, and 555 obviously means a big change.

When you see the number 5 repeated it can also be a wake-up call to make you realise that you need to change something in your life; it may be your home, career, relationship, your diet or even simply your attitude.

There's no need to fear the changes signified by the presence of the number 555. Change can be unsettling at first but ultimately it is very important because it brings in new energy, new beginnings and new life experiences. It is important that you keep a positive mindset during any time of change. The number 5 also represents adventure, freedom, travel and movement. It offers you choices and lets you know that you are not tied down – there is so much moving and changing around you.

If you would like further clarification on which area of your life is about to change, you can ask your spirit guides and angels to show you a sign which relates to the area of change.

Number 6's

Materialism, Imbalance, Re-focusing

It can be unsettling for some people to see the number sequence 666 because there have been some negative superstitions, beliefs and attention associated with this number over the years.

The number sequence of 666 can sometimes indicate that your life is out of balance, and that you are too focused on material things instead of your family and/or your intuition. This sign lets you know that you need to lift your spirits, and surround yourself with positive energy and positive people because you need to re-centre yourself and find balance in your life.

This may also be a sign to get you to look at what you've been spending your money on. Do you really need these extra material goods or do you just want them?

According to numerology, 666 is not a negative number sequence at all; it is all about compassion and helping other people in the community. So if you think this sign may be a prompt for you to think about the way you spend your money, try to shift your focus away from the material world and become more engaged with family, friends and your community.

Number 7's

Miracles, Luck, Dreams coming true

The number 7 is considered a very lucky number by many people, and also a very spiritual number. Congratulations if you have had this number come up because 777 is a wonderful and very positive number sequence and sign – it means that your wishes will come true!

777 also encourages you to become creative, to look within yourself and to trust in your own intuition. This number lets you know that you are being rewarded for all of your hard work and for your positive attitude by your spirit guides and angels.

By showing you the number sequence of 777, your spirit guides and angels are telling you it's time now for you to expect miracles in your life and for you to reap the fruits of your labour. Your reward doesn't always have to be material or financial; it could be that after a period of hard study, you find out you have been accepted into your first choice of university. Or maybe you've been trying to land a particular job and it comes through for you.

Number 8's

Abundance, Health, Happiness

888 is a truly magical number! Seeing it repeated around you is a sign of abundance in your personal life. Abundance can come in many forms, it's not just about financial prosperity, it can also relate to good health, happiness and positive relationships. The number 8 is all about balance; it means that everything is as it should be, so relax, remain positive and enjoy the abundance that will come through for you.

In Chinese culture the number 8 is considered to be very auspicious and lucky. It represents good fortune and good luck, and this energy is tripled in the number sequence of 888, making it a very good omen indeed!

Turned onto its side, the number 8 becomes the symbol for infinity. So this number can also serve as a reminder of the eternal nature of things – there is no beginning and no ending; life just carries on.

The number 8 is also linked with karma, drawing your attention to the spiritual and universal law of cause and effect, which means that whatever energy and intention you send out into the Universe comes back to you threefold.

Number 9's

Endings, New beginnings, De-cluttering

The number 9 or number sequence 999 as signs relate to endings and new beginnings, and herald a time for moving forwards rather than for stagnation.

Whatever 'endings' are taking place around you, know that they are essential because they make way for new beginnings to come through. Trust that everything is happening for a positive reason. The number sequence of 999 is a very powerful number which triples the energy behind the number 9.

When the number 999 appears in your life it can be an encouragement to let go of an aspect of the past to make way for new beginnings and the future. The number 999 doesn't have to always be about dramatic or drastic changes or endings, it can be something small such as leaving a job to start a new one or clearing space and de-cluttering in your home to get rid of stale old energy.

You may need to tie up some old loose ends when you see the number 9 or 999 show up as a sign in your life. There may be some legal matters or outstanding debts that you need to finalise.

Birds

Messages, Communication, Spirit signs

Birds are a sign from spirit; try to take note if they appear on a special day, date or time. When a bird is a spirit sign it will usually appear in an unusual location or it will stare at you and you will feel like it is trying to communicate with you.

Different birds can be signs for different things; you can look up the meanings of some common birds in this book. If you would like to find out more about the specific meaning of each bird, it is best to look at the characteristics of that bird, for example: the Australian kookaburra is about joy and communication because it has a call that sounds like it is laughing.

It is also important to pay attention to the number of birds that are around you and what they are doing. For example if there are two birds that are nesting together this is a sign of positive energy in your relationship and home. If you see some birds that appear to be fighting, you may need to look out for some arguments around you. Or maybe there is a single bird that is trying to give you a message!

Butterfly

Spirit, Transformation, Going within

To see a butterfly is a wonderful thing, especially when you see it randomly in a place where you wouldn't expect to find one. When you see a butterfly it is a sign from your passed loved ones; it means that they are with you and they are very happy and at peace.

Butterflies also symbolise change, new beginnings and transformation, so the next time a butterfly comes close to you or follows you around, it could be a sign the energy of change is present in your life.

The colour of the butterfly can also be significant, so look for patterns in the colour of butterflies you see – you might find that a butterfly of a particular colour appears on more than one occasion when you think of a particular person in spirit.

Another meaning associated with the butterfly as a sign is the need to go within, to nurture yourself while you are going through the process of change, like the caterpillar does. Then when you are ready, you will break out of the old skin and old energy so that you can become the beautiful butterfly.

Clairaudience
Hearing Messages

Hearing, Thinking, Knowing

There are different ways to hear messages from spirit; you may hear the sound, voice or noise with your physical ears or you may hear the noise clairaudiently as a voice or thought in your mind.

Many spirit messages come in the form of you hearing or having a thought. For example if you are choosing between two houses to buy, you may hear in a thought form in your mind, "Buy the first property, it will suit you better." You may not always realise that this may not be your own thought; it could be a spirit message from your passed loved ones or spirit guides.

You can also sometimes hear spirit with your physical hearing sense, it doesn't always have to be in your mind. An example of this could be the sound of a voice yelling your name, or telling you to stop when there is no one else around you.

It doesn't matter which way you receive your messages, just know that these messages are real and they do come in different ways from spirit.

Clairvoyance
Visually Seeing Spirit

Seeing, Feeling, Sensing

It is a sign when you see spirits, shapes and forms with your own physical eyes, or even your third eye (inner mind). When you see with your physical eyes, it may be a form, dark shape or shadow or you may even see a person very clearly as if a real living person was in front of you.

The other way that you may see spirit is with your third eye. This is where you see things with your eyes closed, using your inner eye, your mind. When you see things in this way, it is called using your 'clairvoyance.'

Clairvoyant messages are very common. You may see a sign or symbol that you need to focus upon, or a number, a word, or even a person or animal in spirit that you need to pay attention to. It's important to look further into what you are being shown – sometimes you may be shown the sign very quickly and it is gone in the blink of an eye. If, for example, you are shown an animal in your mind, you may like to look up that animal and see what the spiritual meaning or message behind it is.

Clocks/Watches
Stopping and starting on particular times

Pay attention, Passed loved ones, Time

Clocks and watches can be stopped by spirit in an attempt to get your attention. Often they will stop a number of different clocks/watches so that you realise it is not just due to a faulty timepiece or flat batteries. Each clock may stop at different times but usually it will be all within a short period of time or they may all stop at the same time.

If you do have a clock or watch that has stopped, it's important to note at what time it stopped. Sometimes a clock may stop at the time that a passed loved one of yours passed away. Don't worry if the time is not significant to you, it could also be that spirit has merely stopped the clock to get your attention.

If you keep noticing certain numbers or times appearing on a clock or if you keep waking up at a strange time, for example 3:33 or 11:11, this is a message from spirit. You can look up its meaning in the numbers section towards the beginning of this book.

Clouds
Formations & Shapes

Images, Symbols, Messages

Cloud-gazing is one of the simplest ways to receive messages from your spirit guides and passed loved ones. Clouds can come in all different shapes and sizes. When you look at them you can sometimes make out specific shapes, which may stay for a while or for the briefest of moments. Due to the fleeting nature of clouds, it is easy to overlook a shape or form; on a windy day the shape may be blown away quite quickly before you get a chance to notice it.

If you do see a shape or image in the clouds take time to look at what it means for you, for example if you see a horse-shaped cloud, what does the horse symbolise for you? A horse can mean freedom to some people or if you are a person that loves horses, it could be a passed horse letting you know that it is with you. Often the pictures or shapes you see in the clouds are spirit messages and signs which give you information about what you need to focus upon or what is to come for you in the future.

Coffee / Tea Leaves
Images in the coffee grains or crema & tea leaves

Pictures, Intuition, Prediction

Many people may have heard of the ancient art of reading the leaves at the bottom of a tea cup after a person has finished drinking their tea. It is also possible to read the foam or *crema* that is left over in your cup after having a coffee or hot chocolate. You don't need to be a coffee drinker to be able to read the *crema* left in the cup, and hot chocolate leaves behind its own foamy residue as well.

Try to see if there is an image, a letter, a picture or a symbol that stands out to you when you look into the empty cup. There may even be multiple images or symbols in the one cup. If there is an image there that you are not sure of or a symbol that you can't understand, you may like to write it down or take a photo of it so that you can research what it means. Be sure to trust your own gut instincts and intuition about what it looks like or represents too, as that could be even more significant.

Coins / Jewellery

Good luck, Important dates, Gifts from spirit

You may have heard the old saying, "Find a penny, pick it up and all day you'll have good luck." Well, there is some truth in this. Spirit can give us signs in the form of coins or pieces of jewellery that we find.

If you find a coin in an obscure place, pick it up, have a look and check the year on the coin. Sometimes the year will correspond with an important birthday, anniversary or the passing of a loved one. Now of course it's quite common for coins to be around, people lose loose change all the time, but there are never any coincidences – see if the year does relate to something important. Take special notice if you find the coin in an obscure location.

If you are lucky, you may even find a piece of jewellery. If you find a piece of jewellery that has been lost, whether it belongs to you or to someone else, and it suddenly appears in a very obvious place, this is your passed loved ones helping you. It is a gift from spirit to let you know they are with you.

Crow

Warning, Be alert, Adapt

When you see a crow that is trying to get your attention, it can be a sign of change for you. This is not a negative thing; change is a natural part of life. When the crow shows up in your life, it could be that you need to use your intuition more. It may also be time for you to think outside the box, or adapt to a new situation in your life and move forwards.

Crows are very common; they can be found in many countries around the world. In many different cultures, shamans have used the crow or crow medicine as a symbol of magic and clairvoyance. The crow can also mean that it is time for you to open your intuition and clairvoyance back up, start trusting in your gut feelings again.

In some cultures the crow symbolises that someone is watching over you. The crow can also give you a warning or foretell future events. Crows are very wary birds, they are always on the lookout for danger, and they can communicate with you and warn you if something is not right or you need to look out for something.

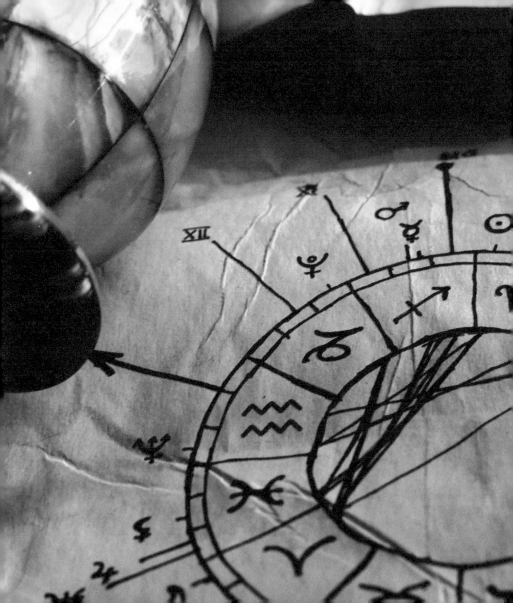

Dates
Births and deaths on the same day, important dates being repeated

Passed loved ones, Synchronicity, Soul links

Sometimes a baby is born into a family shortly following the death of an older family member. This can be seen as the older spirit/person making room for the new spirit/baby to be born. It is also worth paying attention to significant dates – these are often repeated within families and this can be a sign from spirit; for example, when a baby is born on the same date as another loved one's birthday, passing or anniversary. It can be significant even if the person has passed a long time ago – you may have had a loved one pass 20 years earlier and then you have a child or grandchild born on the same birthday as the person who passed.

Dates being repeated do not only have to relate to new births and passings: it can also be a sign when birth dates or important dates are repeated amongst friends, lovers or family members. Pay attention if you share a birth date with someone because this can be a sign that there may be a soul link with that person or a specific reason they are in your life.

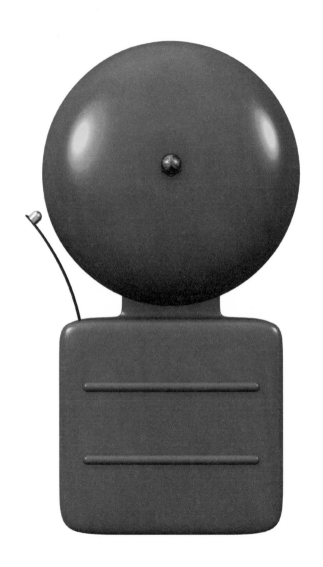

Door Bells / Alarms Bells
Ringing with no batteries in it

Pay attention, Spirit visitation, Trust

Because spirit is made up of pure energy, it's quite easy for spirit to send you signs through electrical devices – they can manipulate that kind of energy easily. If you have a door bell, smoke alarm or security system that keeps going off, and you have checked the batteries or had it looked at and there is no smoke, no one at the door or no intruders around, this may be a spirit sign. It can be your spirit guides or passed loved ones trying to get your attention.

As annoying as it can be to have a loud alarm going off, it really can be a wake-up call from spirit asking you to pay attention or letting you know that they are with you. If you experience a sign like this, notice whether it happens on a particular special day or if it relates to something that is important to you.

Often we don't realise that it was a sign until some time afterwards. Try to think back on times in the past when alarms or electrical items have gone off inexplicably and see how it related to what happened to you around that time.

Dragonfly

Flexibility, Beauty, Strength

Dragonflies are unique – they often seem to appear out of nowhere and quickly flit off to another place. They are not as common as some of the other insects so they do tend to stand out as a sign because they are out of the ordinary.

The message or sign of the dragonfly is similar to that of the butterfly. Dragonflies represent transformation in your life and flexibility. They also let you know that your passed loved ones are with you.

Dragonfly wings are so intricate and delicate, yet they are strong enough to carry the relatively heavy weight of the dragonfly's body. The dragonfly can move swiftly around any obstacles. It comes with a message for you that you can break free from any self-doubt or self-limiting ideas. It is a sign to let your true self come out and shine in full colour!

The dragonfly may have also come into your world to highlight your need for balance in the emotional, mental, spiritual and physical aspects of your life. You may need to ground yourself for a while, to centre yourself before you fly off into the next stage of your life.

Dreams – Spirit Visitations

Support, Communication, Reconnect

Everyone dreams, it's just that some of us don't remember our dreams the next day. However there is a big difference between a spirit dream/ spirit visitation and a normal dream.

In a spirit dream/visitation you can feel and remember the dream when you wake up and sometimes the feeling can stay with you for months or years. In the dream, you may have been visited by a passed loved one/ animal or a spirit guide. You will feel like you are actually physically with the person/being. Often you may not remember the exact conversation that you have in the dream but you will remember the feelings.

Spirit sometimes likes to throw a random weird thing into the dream to be sure that you remember it. It could be the setting of the dream or a peculiar person or animal in the dream with you.

Remember that it is the energy of the dream that is important. Your passed loved ones or spirit guides are trying to get through you. You may be so busy during the day that this is the only way they can reach you, when you are asleep.

Dream Symbols

Messages, Information, Higher self

Dreams are a very important way that spirit can get messages or signs through to you. Not every dream will have a message in it, but there will be some dreams that you remember that will give you information from your spirit guides, passed loved ones and even your higher self.

If you pay attention to your dreams, you will gain insight that is specifically designed to help you progress in your life.

It is important that you look at all aspects of the dream. Who is in the dream – is it a family member, a friend, a stranger or perhaps someone famous? What is happening in the dream? What emotions are associated with it? Where is the dream is taking place? Are there are any significant animals or objects in the dream?

When you start to look at your dreams, it's a new way to interpret messages from your higher self and your guides. There are many different books and resources on the internet that list the specific dream meanings and symbology: find the meaning that best resonates with you.

Eagle

Higher perspective, Right path, Connection

Eagles soar high above the Earth, seeing everything from a higher perspective. If you look at things from an eagle's viewpoint, you can see more easily how to deal with issues in your life because you're not stuck on the ground, surrounded by trees.

The eagle also connects heaven and earth; it is the messenger that takes your prayers and thoughts to the spirit world. Even though eagles soar at great heights above the ground, they still remain connected to the earth. This is an important spiritual lesson for us: we need to fly high but remain grounded at the same time.

If you see an eagle flying in front of you, particularly when you're travelling or driving, this is a great sign that you are on the right path. It is also a sign from spirit confirming that they are with you, supporting you during the trip or in whatever you are dealing with at the time.

If an eagle soars above you in the sky this is a great sign to remind you that you are not alone and also an encouragement to reach higher and extend yourself – don't limit yourself.

Electrical Appliances
Kettles, Lamps, Microwaves, Ovens & more

Information, Be aware, Spirit visitation

It may seem a bit strange that spirit would use everyday appliances such as kettles, microwaves and even radios to get a sign or message through to someone but it does happen.

Have you ever had an electric jug turn itself on when no one is else is around? Or a microwave whose clock keeps stopping at a particular time or that turns itself off and back on? Maybe even a radio that keeps changing radio stations by itself or whose volume keeps getting turned up and down? Spirit may even turn the radio on at just the right time for you to hear a significant song or piece of useful information.

If all of the above happened at the same time it may be a little bit frightening to some people, so usually only one thing occurs at a time because spirit does not do this to scare you.

Spirit may manipulate appliances to get your attention or to let you know that a loved one is with you, for example if your passed mother loved to have a cup of tea, she may turn the electric jug on as her sign for you that she is still with you.

Feathers

Angels, You're not alone, Confirmation

Often feathers will appear out of nowhere. A single feather may fall from the sky, appear next to you or blow across your path. Feathers are a common sign that people receive from their angels and passed loved ones. Sometimes the feather is sent to you just to confirm that you are not alone and that you are on the right track.

Try to pay attention when you do see a single feather and thank your angels, spirit guides and passed loved ones. If you do find a feather you may like to keep it as a reminder that you are not alone and that spirit is with you.

Feathers come in all different colours and shapes – you might find a beautiful pristine white one, a black and white larger feather or even a small brown speckled one. You may constantly find feathers of the same kind and colour or you may find completely different ones. Take note of the colour of your feather. White feathers can represent angels, whereas coloured or black and white feathers can be from your spirit guides.

Flowers / Plants

Anniversaries, Birthdays, Passed loved ones

Every flower is unique and beautiful in its own way and scented ones are especially wonderful! This may be why spirit often uses flowers as signs. An example of this is if you find a flower unexpectedly in front of you on the footpath, reminding you of your favourite person or passed loved one.

Another spirit sign is when a seemingly dead rose bush or flower patch at a person's home sprouts back to life with the most amazing flowers, as if by magic. Often these flowers will bloom on a special day such as a birthday, anniversary or on Mothers' day. The interesting thing is that this can occur even when it is not the right season for that flower. The same thing can happen with fruit trees or vegetable patches.

Many people may think that this is a coincidence, but there are simply too many stories like this for it to be so. Here's an example from my experience: there was a lemon tree in my garden that had not borne fruit for many years. After the passing of a person close to me who loved lemons, the tree suddenly produced an abundance of beautifully shaped fruit – yes, this is definitely a sign from the spirit world!

Frogs

Rebirth, Fertility, Good luck

It is rare for frogs to be seen out in the open; they have very delicate skin which needs to be protected from chemicals and the sun. Whether you see a frog in your letter box, your laundry, your toilet or near your car, it is an important sign.

When a frog appears in your life, it is a sign for you to look at what area of your life is undergoing a transition in your life. The appearance of a frog can signify a time of new beginnings and rebirth.

In some cultures, the frog is a sign of abundance and fertility due to their prolific egg-laying. In Japan, frogs are considered lucky for travellers, it is common to give someone who is preparing to travel a small frog token so that they have a safe trip. You can also put a small frog token in your purse or wallet so that money will not be lost.

Frogs can also be a sign that rain is coming – they can start to croak loudly up to 24 hours before a lot of wet weather sets in.

Lights
Turning on and off, flickering

Correct thinking, Keep going, Validation

We have all experienced the power or the lights going out but when spirit turns the lights on and off, it is very different to a normal power outage or a bulb or fuse blowing.

Spirit can easily turn lights off or on or make them flicker, and this can happen at home, work, anywhere. They may do this just as you are thinking of a passed loved one, in confirmation that the thought is being received. It can also be a way to get your attention and let you know you are not alone – but it's not designed to scare you!

Some people have experienced the lights flickering so much that they worry that the wiring in their home is faulty. When they have their wiring checked by an electrician, it often turns out that there is nothing wrong with it.

Pay attention also when you notice the street lights turn off or flicker as you are driving. If this happens at an unusual time and cannot be explained by the timers that cause street lights to come on as night falls, it is spirit specifically choosing to make that happen at that time to get your attention.

Music
Significant songs or favourite songs
of passed loved ones

Questions answered, Passed loved ones, Remember

Signs from spirit frequently come through music. Often passed loved ones will use music or songs to let you know that they are around you. You might notice the person's favourite song being played on the radio repeatedly even though it could be quite an old song.

If you have a particular song that reminds you of a passed loved one and you notice it suddenly keeps being played, this is a sign from them to let you know you are still connected. (You may need to use your own judgement and common sense here; if it is a current top ten hit that would be played all the time anyway, it may not be significant, it just depends on the situation.) There may even be a song that keeps coming up that says your loved one's name or something that relates to you both together.

Another way that music is a sign is when you hear a particular song that answers a question that you may have in your mind. For example, if you're wondering whether you should call someone and then a song comes on the radio called with the lyrics, "Call me, baby," it can be a confirmation that you should make the phone call.

HELLO
my name is

Names
Names being repeated, getting called out

Spirit message, Warning, Connection

Names being repeated are a very strong sign from spirit – this often occurs in threes. You may get signs by seeing the name of a loved one repeated within a short amount of time. For example you watch a TV show and the main character is called your loved one's name, then you go for a drive and on the radio you hear someone with the same name as your loved one. The third sign may be as simple as hearing someone calling out to someone with the same name as your loved one. This is an example of three very strong signs making you aware your passed loved one is with you or that you need to connect with a living loved one.

Another way spirit can use names as a sign is when they have to warn you of something. An example of this is when you're about to cross a busy street, you may hear someone shout out your name. You stop to see who it is and no one is there, but you realise then that if you hadn't stopped you could have crossed the road and been hit by the car that sped around the corner at that same moment.

Number Plates

Important information, Clues, Specific details

Pay attention as you travel around on the roads – there are signs all around you. Notice the logos and stickers on the vehicles near you, look at the names and numbers to see if there is anything significant for you. For example, if you need direction about whether to sell your home, you might ask for a sign to help you decide. After you ask, you may be driving and notice that there are two cars next to you in traffic and both cars have real estate logos on them. This may be a sign that yes, it is time for you to consider selling your home.

It's also very important that you look at number plates – they can deliver signs in various ways. The numbers could relate to important dates for you. Seeing repeated numbers might inspire you to look up what they mean. If you see the number plate '555LUV', it may mean there will be change (555 represents change) and LUV could mean the change relates your love life. The letters and combinations on number plates can relate to very specific things as well – it is up to you to look deeper into the meanings and make the connections that relate to your situation.

Orbs

Special events, Sacred sites, Spiritual areas

Spirit orbs are circles of light that appear unexpectedly in photos after the photo has been taken. Orbs have been captured a lot more recently due to the higher resolution of images and ever-improving quality of digital cameras nowadays. Often people may think these orbs are just fragments of light from the sun or smudges on the camera – this can happen too but spirit orbs are a sign from spirit and your passed loved ones to let you know they are with you.

Usually the orbs are located around the heart, or in the head or shoulder area. Have a look at photos that you have taken to see if there are any orbs in them. Look especially at photos from important events such as weddings, christenings and birthdays. Also look at who the orbs are near, and how the event relates to that person because that can give you a clue as to who that spirit orb is in spirit and why that spirit is there.

Orbs can also be seen floating around in photos of sacred sites and/or places of significance where many people are known to have passed.

Owl

Magic, Clairvoyance, Wisdom

Traditionally owls have been linked to magic and clairvoyance. If you are lucky enough to have an owl visit you, know that this is a very positive sign.

In some Native American tribes the owl is a strong protector. Owl feathers were used and worn to keep away the evil spirits. Owls represent wisdom, teaching, protection, prophecy and intuition.

The owl has also been known as a sign of death in some cultures. This does not necessarily mean someone physically dying. It can mean the death of a situation, new beginnings and transition. If this applies to you, look at what is ending around you, and focus on transitioning and moving forward.

In other cultures the owl represents a warning. You may need to stop, watch and listen. Try to be discreet, don't be too forthcoming in your plans, and keep the details to yourself for a while. Take time to observe what is going on around you. You may need to spend some time alone and meditate to connect with your own intuition.

Pets
Domestic Pets Communicating with Spirit

Instinct, Loyalty, Telepathy

Animals are naturally instinctive, and they have the ability to see and sense spirits. If you have ever had a pet dog or cat, you may have noticed how they intuitively know when you are sad or not feeling well – they will often come close to you and try to offer support just with their presence. Pets are in many ways great healers.

Sometimes the link between pets and owners is very strong. There is often a kind of companion soul mate connection where both the pet and the owner are deeply connected on a spiritual and emotional level. This link does not break or disappear after the owner or the pet passes, it continues on.

Pets can also help you to sense your loved ones that are in spirit. They are great indicators, and can let you know that there is a spirit person around you. Your pet may bark at nothing in particular or stare at a particular spot in your house and you know that there is nothing else physically there or they may constantly keep walking around and around a particular area trying to get your attention.

Physical Body Signs
Heat, Tingling, Hair raised

Sensing, Awareness, Confirmation

You may have experienced the hair on your arms standing up or the hair on your head feeling like it is tingly or being tickled. Another strong sign is a sudden feeling of heat on your body even on a cold day. These physical signs are designed to make you pay attention or to confirm what you are sensing.

Often people also feel icy cold instantly in a particular part of a house or room when they are having an experience with spirit. The temperature can seem to drop suddenly for no particular reason and it may be in just one area of a room. Often this is a sign that spirit is present around you or in that area.

There are so many different physical sensations you can feel that are unexplainable. These signs are particularly strong because it is a physical manifestation of a sign that proves to you that something out of the ordinary is happening. You cannot make yourself feel these signs, they are beyond your control, which is why they feel especially powerful.

Predictive Dreams / Premonitions

Warning, Look deeper, Information provided

Many people experience predictive dreams or have premonitions. Through these, spirit can alert you to something or grab your attention. A predictive dream can be hard to decipher because it is made up of symbols or sequences that you have to work through and their meaning can be very subjective and difficult to interpret. It is often hard to identify a predictive dream until something in the dream manifests in reality – you may have a dream about a baby being born and only realise a few weeks later that it was a premonition when you find out a family member is pregnant.

It's important that you pay attention to your dreams to try to identify any information they may be offering you about your future. It could be something as simple as you being shown a holiday destination to focus on, or your dream could be flagging an important health concern that needs attention. There is often valuable information to be gleaned from dreams, it just takes a conscious effort to look for the signs hidden within them.

Rainbows

New beginnings, Good luck, Positivity

Not only are rainbows beautiful to look at, their presence is uplifting and healing. Seeing a rainbow after a storm or even when it is still raining is a wonderful sign to remind you to look on the bright side of life and acknowledge its beauty and magic. When you take time out to really look at a rainbow it allows you to appreciate what is around you and to be grateful for everything in your life.

Rainbows bring something new into your life in the form of a positive change, such as a new career opportunity, new beginnings in your relationship area or just a new positive energy or starting point.

You are very lucky if you see a double rainbow because it is a double blessing, a double positive hit which lifts your personal life and allows you to see clearly again especially after a draining or depressing time.

Shooting Stars

Wish coming true, Dreams, Destiny

Seeing a shooting star is a very positive sign; it can symbolise the fulfilment of a wish, dreams coming true and even reaching an important part of your destiny. When you see a shooting star it can also mean that there will be a birth in the family or you will have some positive new changes in your life – a kind of rebirth for yourself.

It is very special to see a shooting star in the city because pollution and excessive lighting can make the stars very difficult to see.

Within the ancient Chinese practice of Feng Shui there are many different beliefs associated with seeing a shooting star: if you have been unlucky or unwell, it can mean you will get well and your luck will turn around. It is also believed that when you see a shooting star, whatever you wish for will manifest within the next thirty days. Seeing a shooting star also bodes very well for your relationship area and if you have had an argument with someone, it will be resolved.

Smells

Be aware, Passed loved ones, Familiarity

One of the most common signs people experience is smelling a scent that they relate to a passed loved one. The smell or scent may be their passed loved one's favourite perfume or it may be what they liked to eat, drink or smoke.

Spirit likes to use scent or smells as a sign because it is something that you can't doubt – you can't make yourself smell something if it isn't there. When you smell a particular scent as a sign from spirit, it will happen in a situation where that smell is unusual or unexpected in the setting. If you're alone and you notice a particular smell reminding you of someone, you can be sure it's a sign from spirit.

Smell and scents do not have to only relate to passed loved ones. If you smell a very strong bad odour, it could be that spirit is trying to warn you about something. The smell can sometimes be so awful it is guaranteed to make you stop and pay attention. If you have ever experienced this you would know it is a smell that cannot be described. Once you smell it though, you automatically know to be aware, it is a very strong sign.

Snakes

Fertility, Life force, Healing

A snake is a very powerful sign; it will get your attention but it is not to be feared. The snake is a well-known symbol of fertility, life force and healing. That's why the snake is featured on the caduceus – the symbol of two snakes wound around a staff – it is the symbol for doctors and physicians in many western countries.

Snakes are known to shed their old skin, so seeing a snake could be a sign that you need to start to move out of your comfort zone, leave the past behind you and shed your old skin (old energy). Focus on leaving behind any old habits or negative behaviours that no longer serve you. Be gentle with yourself if you are transforming and shedding the old energy – everything takes time, there is no rush.

In some spiritual cultures the snake is a symbol of the kundalini/life force energy – the energy that is coiled at the base of your spine. When the kundalini energy is awakened and moves through your body, it is a joining of the masculine and feminine energies which opens up and balances you physically, emotionally, sexually and spiritually.

Spider / Spider Web

Focus, Create, Past and future

Whether you are scared of spiders or not, they are sure to get your attention when you come across them; they are a strong sign from spirit. Spiders represent the feminine and creative energy in many cultures. The spider is said to create and weave the past and the future. It highlights the need for you to create your own destiny. If you have had a spider show up in a peculiar place near you or spiders keep appearing around you, think about what you would like to weave for your future.

Even spider webs can be a sign. A web may be placed across a doorway or in your path to try to make you stop and think about where you are going and what you need to focus upon. Just as it takes the spider time to weave its web, this sign may mean that you need to slow down, take your time and really focus on what your next step is. You cannot rush making a web, you must think about all of the different aspects, or parts of your life that you need to take into consideration.

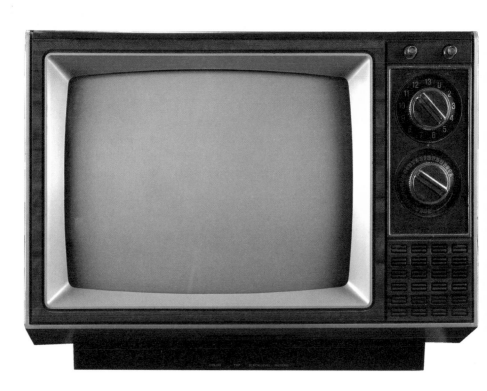

Televisions
Television Credits and Shows with Meanings

Important information, Pay attention, Name confirmations

Televisions are a source of entertainment for people of all ages but they are also a great vessel for spirit to deliver signs to us because items that use electricity can be easily manipulated by spirit to get their message across.

Spirit can deliver signs through the television in many different ways: they can turn your television on and off and they may even turn the television's volume up and down to try to get your attention.

Sometimes you may have a feeling that you need to turn on the television and just at that moment a newsflash will come up with a warning that is relevant to you or a television show will come on with exactly the information you need at that time.

Pay attention to what is on the television when you feel like you are being lead there for a reason. Are you being lead to particular channel at a certain time or to a show that may interest you?

Signs don't only appear in the content of the television programs, you may also get a sign from the names of the characters or even from the real names of the actors in the credits at the end.

Spirit Signs – Keywords

Number Zero – Connection, Manifestation, Eternity
Number One – Confirmation, New beginnings, Synchronicity
Number Two – Balance, Positivity, Partnerships
Number Three – Angels, Spirit guides, Triple trinity
Number Four – Security, Strong foundations, Hard work
Number Five – Change, Transformation, New energy
Number Six – Materialism, Imbalance, Re-focusing
Number Seven – Miracles, Luck, Dreams coming true
Number Eight – Abundance, Health, Happiness
Number Nine – Endings, New beginnings, De-cluttering
Birds – Messages, Communication, Spirit signs
Butterfly – Spirit, Transformation, Going Within
Clairaudience – Hearing, Thinking, Knowing
Clairvoyance – Seeing, Feeling, Sensing
Clocks / Watches – Pay attention, Passed loved ones, Time
Clouds – Images, Symbols, Messages
Coffee / Tea Leaves – Pictures, Intuition, Prediction
Coins / Jewellery – Good luck, Important dates, Gifts from spirit
Crow – Warning, Be alert, Adapt
Dates – Passed loved ones, Synchronicity, Soul links
Door bells / Alarms – Pay attention, Spirit visitation, Trust
Dragonfly – Flexibility, Beauty, Strength
Dreams / Spirit Visitations – Support, Communication, Reconnect

Dream Symbols – Messages, Information, Higher self
Eagle – Higher perspective, Right path, Connection
Electrical Appliances – Information, Be aware, Spirit visitation
Feathers – Angels, You're not alone, Confirmation
Flowers / Plants – Anniversaries, Birthdays, Passed loved ones
Frogs – Rebirth, Fertility, Good Luck
Lights – Correct thinking, Keep going, Validation
Music – Questions answered, Passed loved ones, Remember
Names – Spirit message, Warning, Connection
Number Plates – Important information, Clues, Specific details
Orbs – Special events, Sacred sites, Spiritual areas
Owls – Magic, Clairvoyance, Wisdom
Pets – Instinct, Loyalty, Telepathy
Physical Body Signs – Sensing, Awareness, Confirmation
Predictive / Premonition Dreams – Warning, Look deeper, Information provided
Rainbows – New beginnings, Good luck, Positivity
Shooting Stars – Wish coming true, Dreams, Destiny
Smells – Be aware, Passed loved ones, Familiarity
Snakes – Fertility, Life force, Healing
Spider / Spider Web – Focus, Create, Past and future
Televisions – Important information, Pay attention, Name confirmations

About the Author

Jade-Sky is a Psychic/Medium – a 'direct channeller.' Gifted with the ability to connect clairvoyantly with energies of deceased loved ones, over the past 22 years, Jade-Sky has been fine-tuning her natural skills in the areas of psychometry, mediumship/channelling and uncovering past lives. Jade-Sky has read professionally for clients from all around the world.

Mediumship is Jade-Sky's passion. She offers private consultations in which she connects to the inquirer's passed loved ones, providing very personal and significant details to help clients truly feel and experience the connection which often helps immensely with the grieving process.

The interpretation of signs and symbols from spirit is an important part of Jade-Sky's work as a medium and she has a wealth of knowledge and experience in this field, which she is honoured to share with you in this book.

Jade-Sky gives retreats and workshops across Australia and internationally and is a regular speaker at Mind Body Spirit events.

In 2012, Jade was named Australian Psychic of the Year (Queensland).

www.jade-sky.com.au

For more information on this
or any Blue Angel Publishing release,
please visit our website at:

www.blueangelonline.com